We Are The People –

Coloring Book

Color these designs & more!

ALSO BY **SHUINA SKO**

BScAppPsy

COLORING BOOKS

We Are The People – Naat A Maklaks – Coloring Book

POETRY BOOKS

Love Me (With Angel Lena)
Frybread Power
You Are Not Alone
Her Love
Heart Poems for the Hopeless Romantic
She is Matriarch
Two-Spirit Journeying
Big Love – mo stinta
Warrior Roses

We Are The People
Naat A Maklaks

Coloring
Book

Designs From The
Ewksiknii Homelands

SHUINA SKO

WRITTEN & ILLUSTRATED BY SHUINA SKO
CHILOQUIN, OREGON 97624

For information about permission to
reproduce selections from this book, contact
Shuína at www.ShuinaSko.com

Cover photo: Designed by Shuína Skó

Illustrations: Designed by Shuína Skó

Names: Skó, Shuína, author

Title: We Are The People – Naat A Maklaks – Coloring Book:
Designs From The Ewksiknii Homelands

Description: First edition

Paperback Book Identifiers:
ISBN: 9798312467772

This coloring book is
dedicated to the children of
the Klamath, Modoc, &
Northern Paiute

NOTE:

The word *ewksiknii* means people of the marsh, river, and lake in *maklaksyalank hemkanga* (speaking the Klamath language). This word is used interchangeably with "Klamath" when referring to the Klamath nation, which is a federally recognized Indigenous nation on the west side of Turtle Island. The Klamath (ewksiknii) nation is made up of the Klamath, Modoc, and Northern Paiute people.

Contents

Traditional Basket Designs

Introduction

Coloring Creations

digaaga čoog

Traditional Quail Basket Design
CONNECTION | UNITY | COMMUNITY
Representative of the most powerful thunder that carries
restoration and greater wellness

y'ayn'ač & loo

Traditional Mountain & Goose Basket Design
TOGETHERNESS | STRENGTH | HARMONY
Representative of place to obtain spiritual power, insight, & guidance
& providing a secure path in moving forward in a good way

gaagm s'kol'anč

Traditional Crow's Knee Basket Design
HEALING | HOPEFULNESS | HELPING
Representative of the strong yaamas (north wind) that carries warm weather
& supporting growth, healing, and the awakening of life

Introduction

This book contains 75 coloring creations; designs created by Shuína Skó, citizen of the ewksiknii nation, inspired by their ewksiknii culture and the traditional basket designs of their ancestors.

The creations highlight three distinct basket designs: quail, mountain or goose, and the crow's knee.

They also include several significant plants and animals that are valuable relations of the ewksiknii: bear, buffalo, butterfly, deer, frog, hummingbird, coyote, quail, eagle, cedar, sage, wocas (pond lily), and the sugar pinecone.

The ewksiknii are an inherently creative, innovative, and adaptive community with incredibly talented artists, singers, dancers, musicians, entrepreneurs, storytellers, educators, and leaders.

This coloring book is a testament of the vibrant Spirit within each Indigenous person and their ancestors' resilience and courage who preceded them.

This photograph pictures
Shuína's great-great-grandmother Nettie
Ninrod-Wright, an ewksiknii matriarch, and
her daughter wearing traditional regalia and
baskets (made with tule) as head coverings.
Nettie was three when the Klamath
Treaty was signed in 1864.

Coloring Creations

We Are The People – Naat A Maklaks

We Are The People – Naat A Maklaks

We Are The People – Naat A Maklaks

We Are The People – Naat A Maklaks

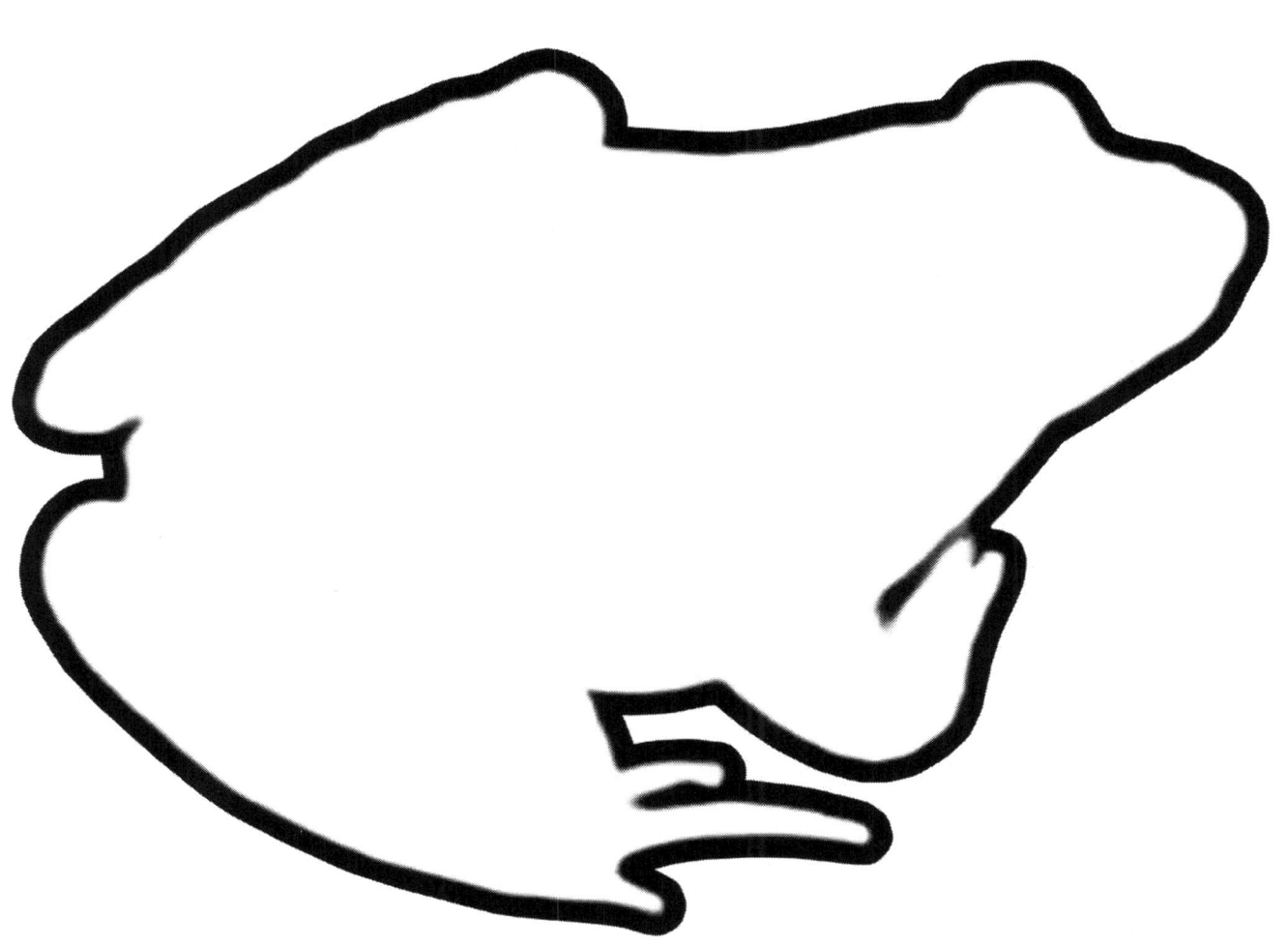

We Are The People – Naat A Maklaks

We Are The People – Naat A Maklaks

We Are The People – Naat A Maklaks

We Are The People – Naat A Maklaks

We Are The People – Naat A Maklaks

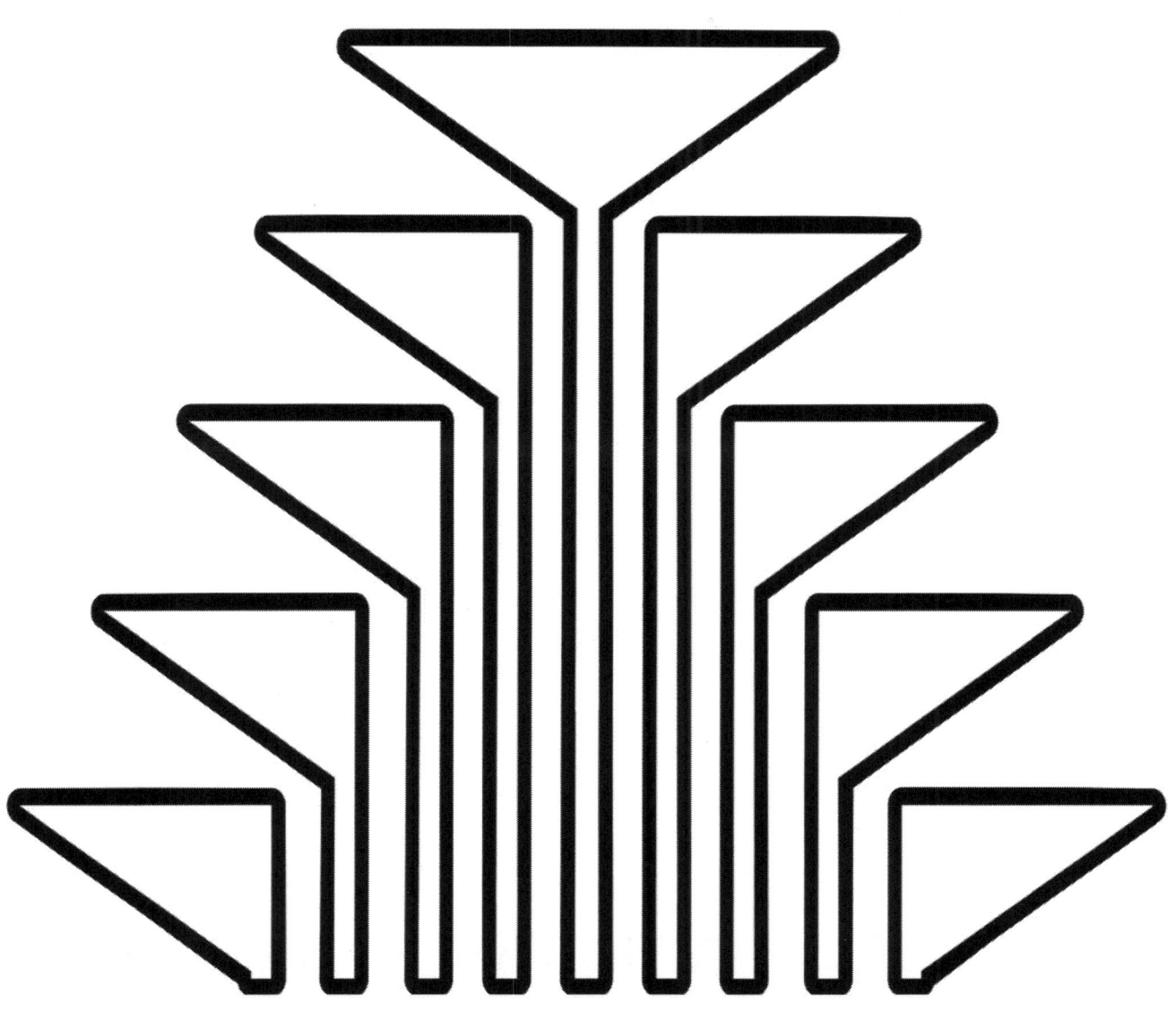

We Are The People – Naat A Maklaks

We Are The People – Naat A Maklaks

We Are The People – Naat A Maklaks

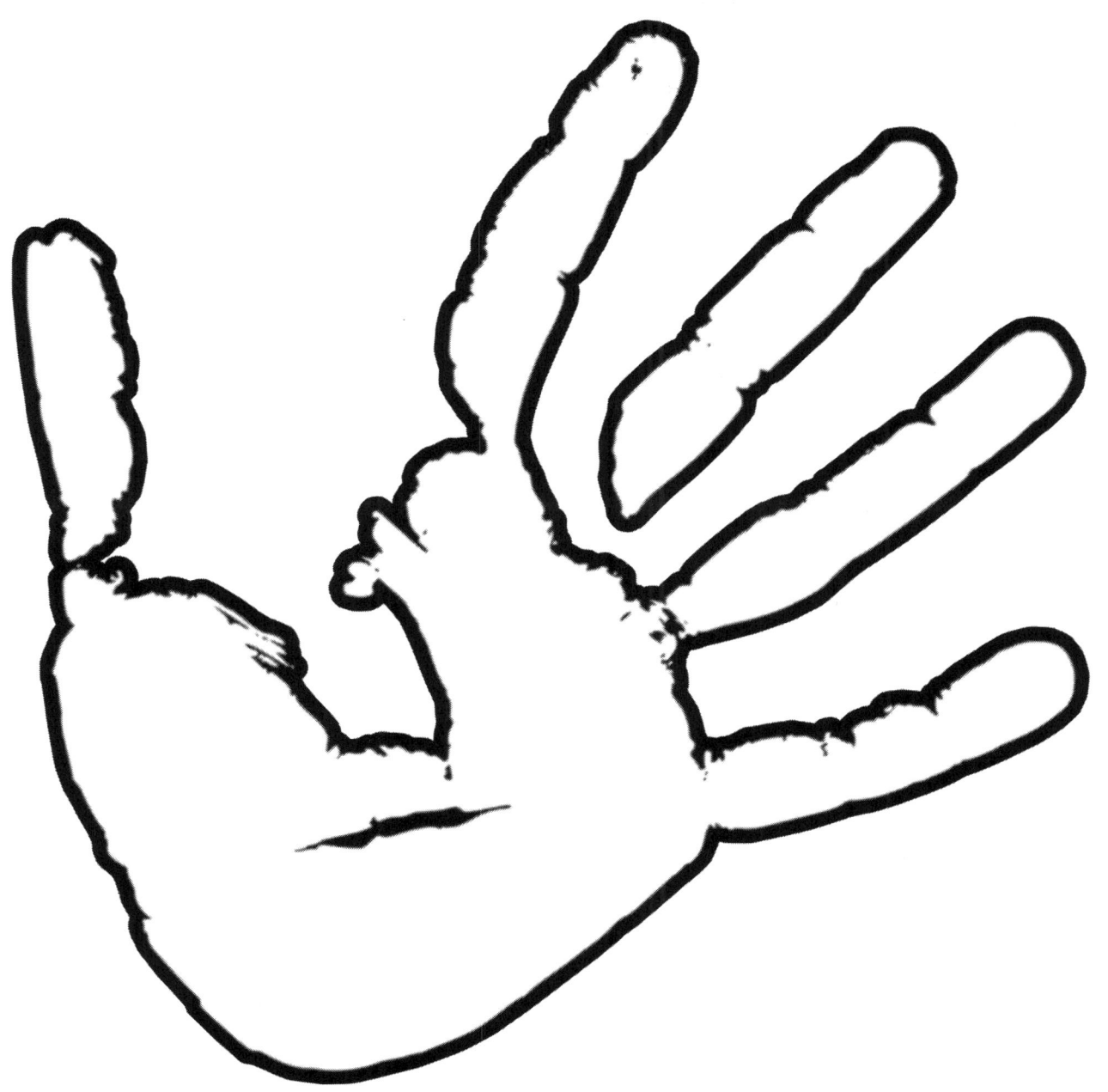

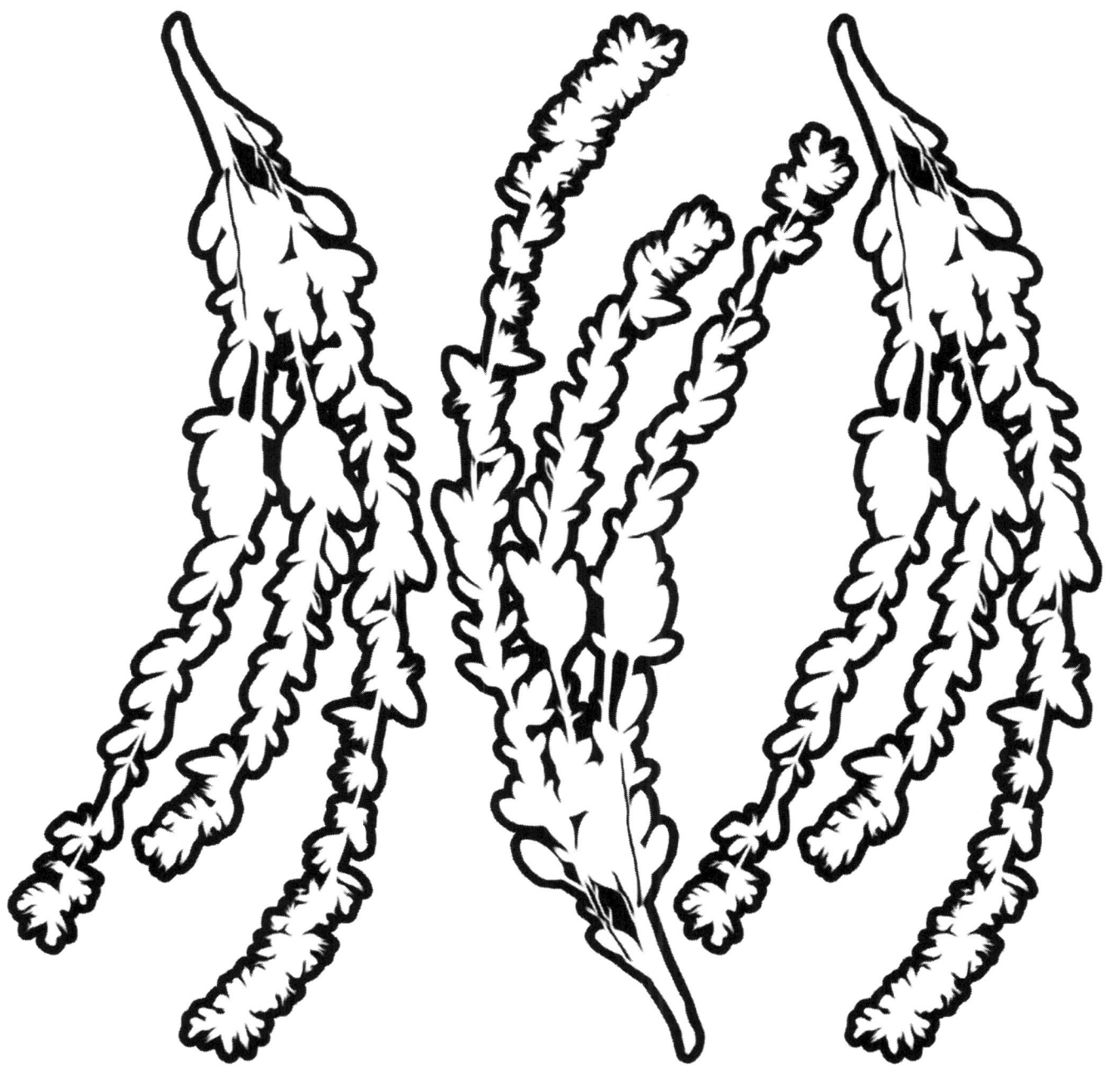

We Are The People – Naat A Maklaks

We Are The People – Naat A Maklaks

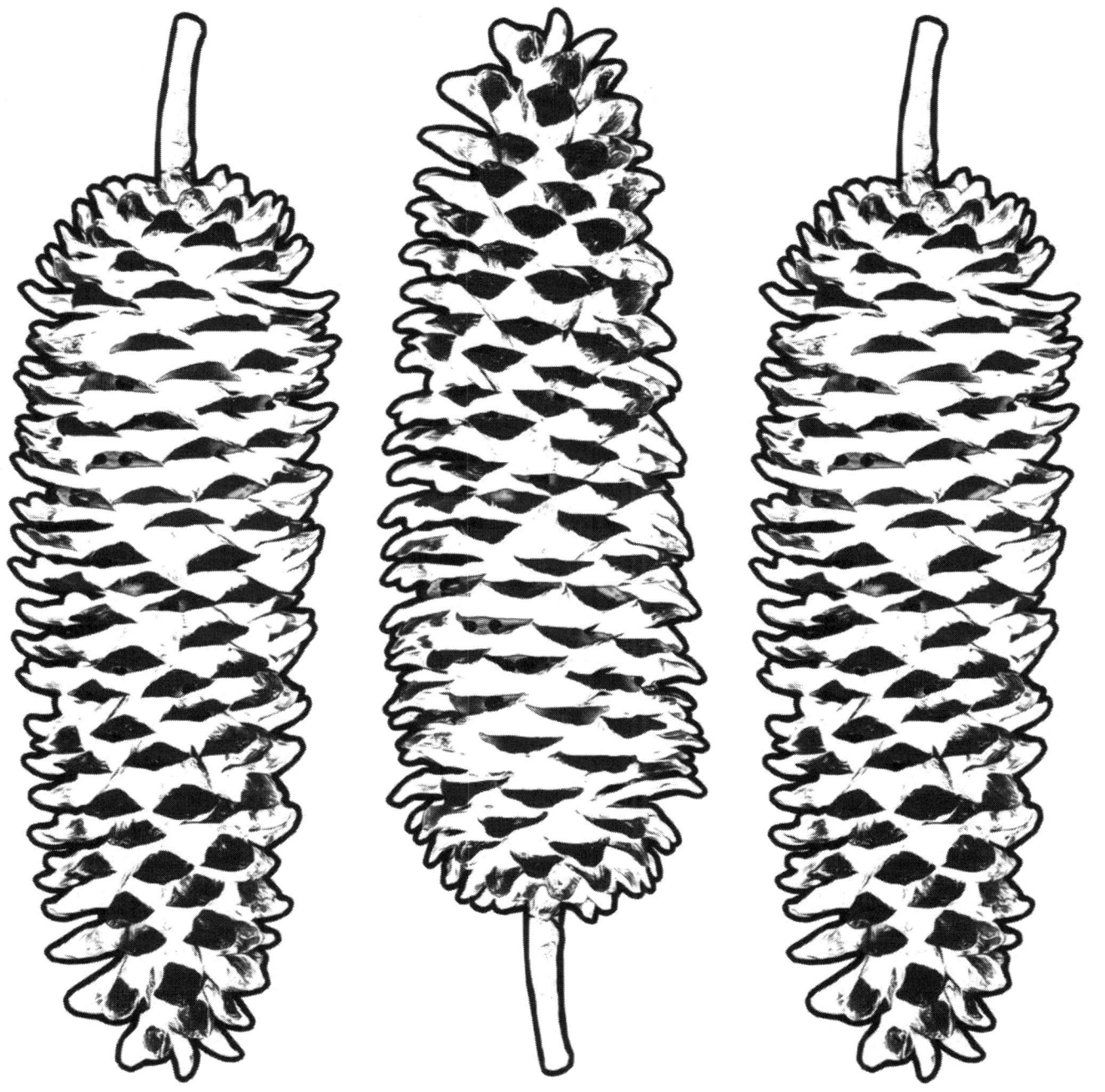

We Are The People – Naat A Maklaks

We Are The People – Naat A Maklaks

We Are The People – Naat A Maklaks

We Are The People – Naat A Maklaks

We Are The People – Naat A Maklaks

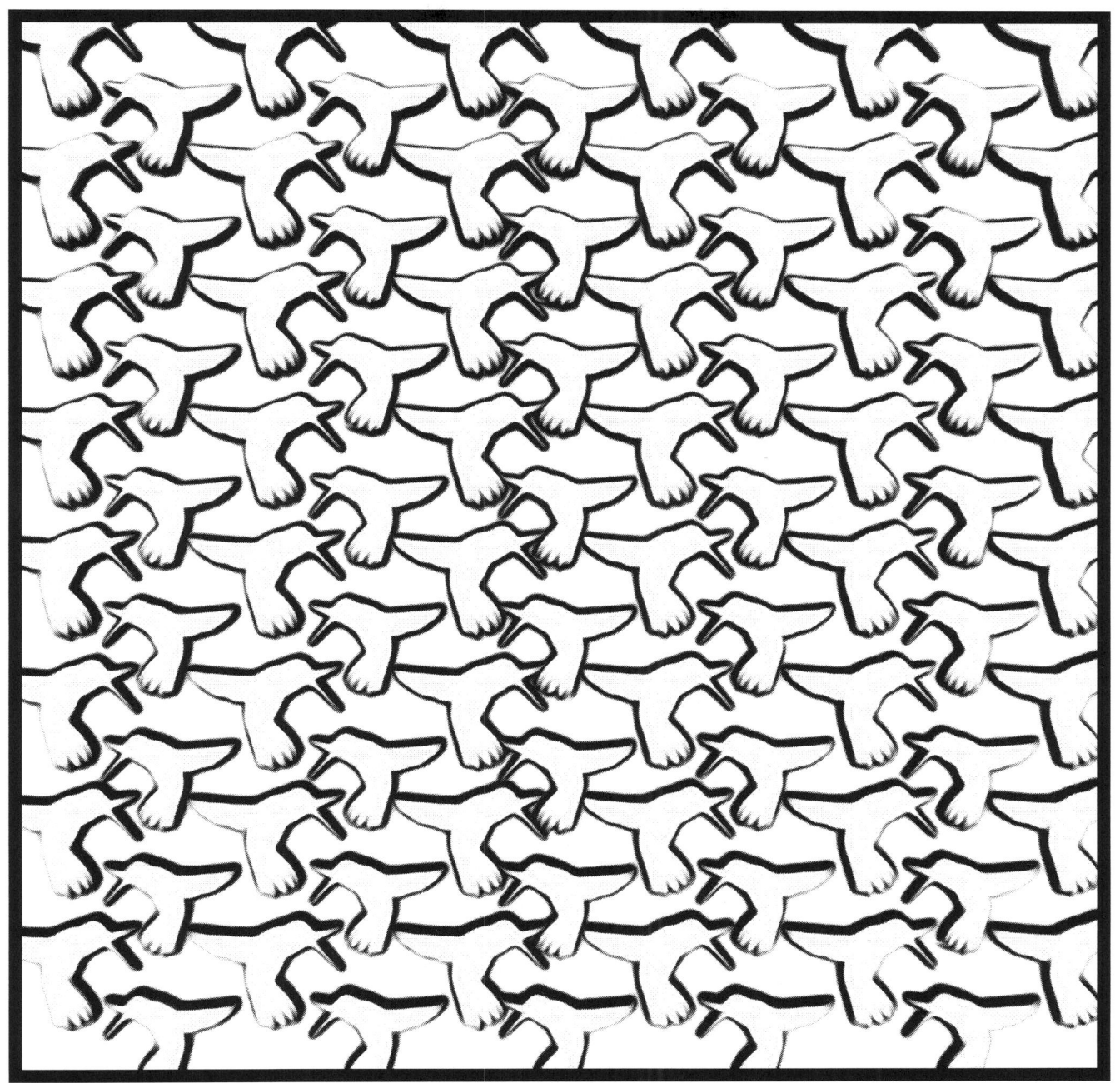

We Are The People – Naat A Maklaks

We Are The People – Naat A Maklaks

We Are The People – Naat A Maklaks

We Are The People – Naat A Maklaks

We Are The People – Naat A Maklaks

We Are The People – Naat A Maklaks

We Are The People – Naat A Maklaks

We Are The People – Naat A Maklaks

We Are The People – Naat A Maklaks

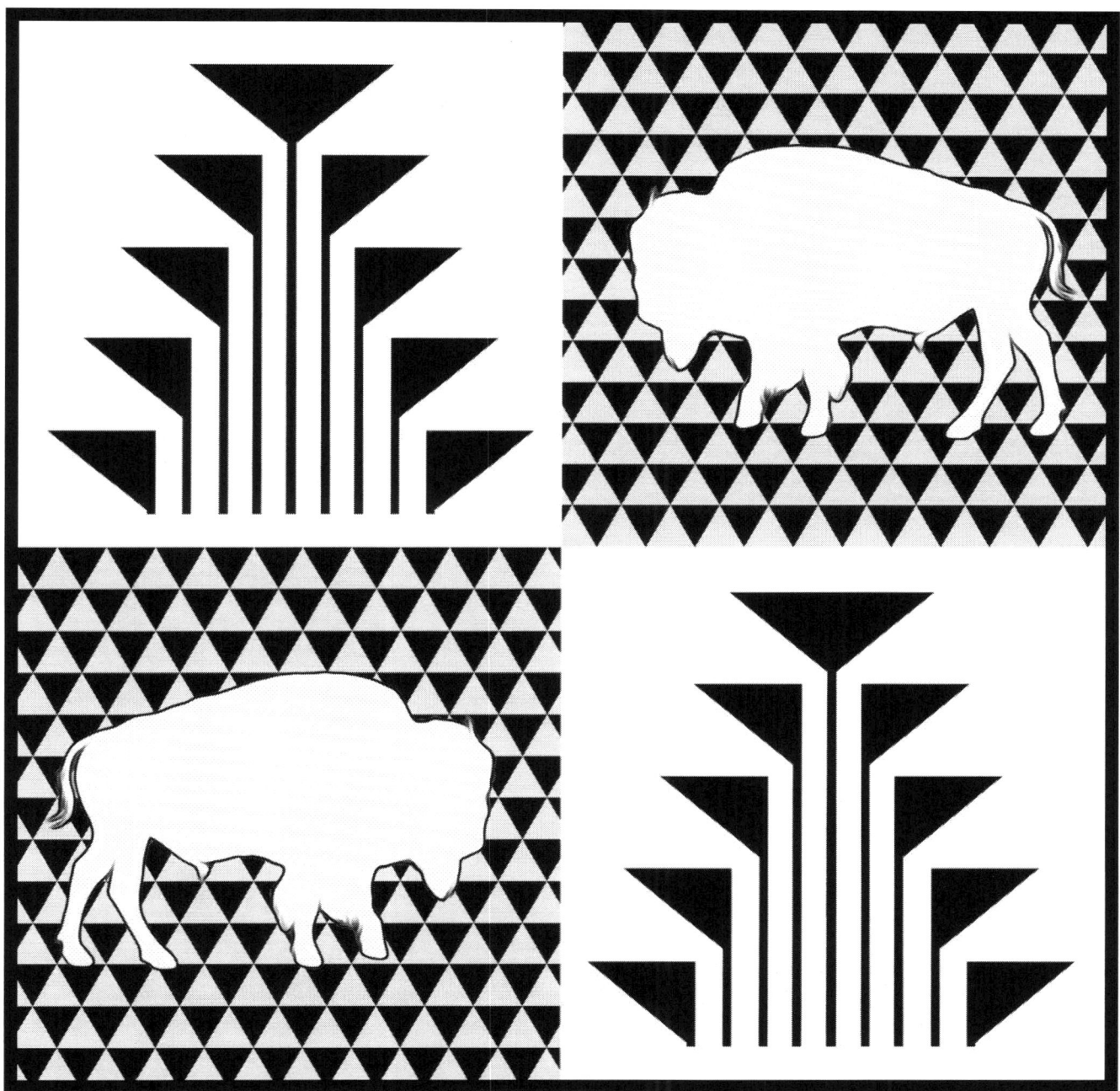

We Are The People – Naat A Maklaks

We Are The People – Naat A Maklaks

We Are The People – Naat A Maklaks

We Are The People – Naat A Maklaks

We Are The People – Naat A Maklaks

We Are The People – Naat A Maklaks

We Are The People – Naat A Maklaks

We Are The People – Naat A Maklaks

We Are The People – Naat A Maklaks

We Are The People – Naat A Maklaks

We Are The People – Naat A Maklaks

We Are The People – Naat A Maklaks

We Are The People – Naat A Maklaks

We Are The People – Naat A Maklaks

We Are The People – Naat A Maklaks

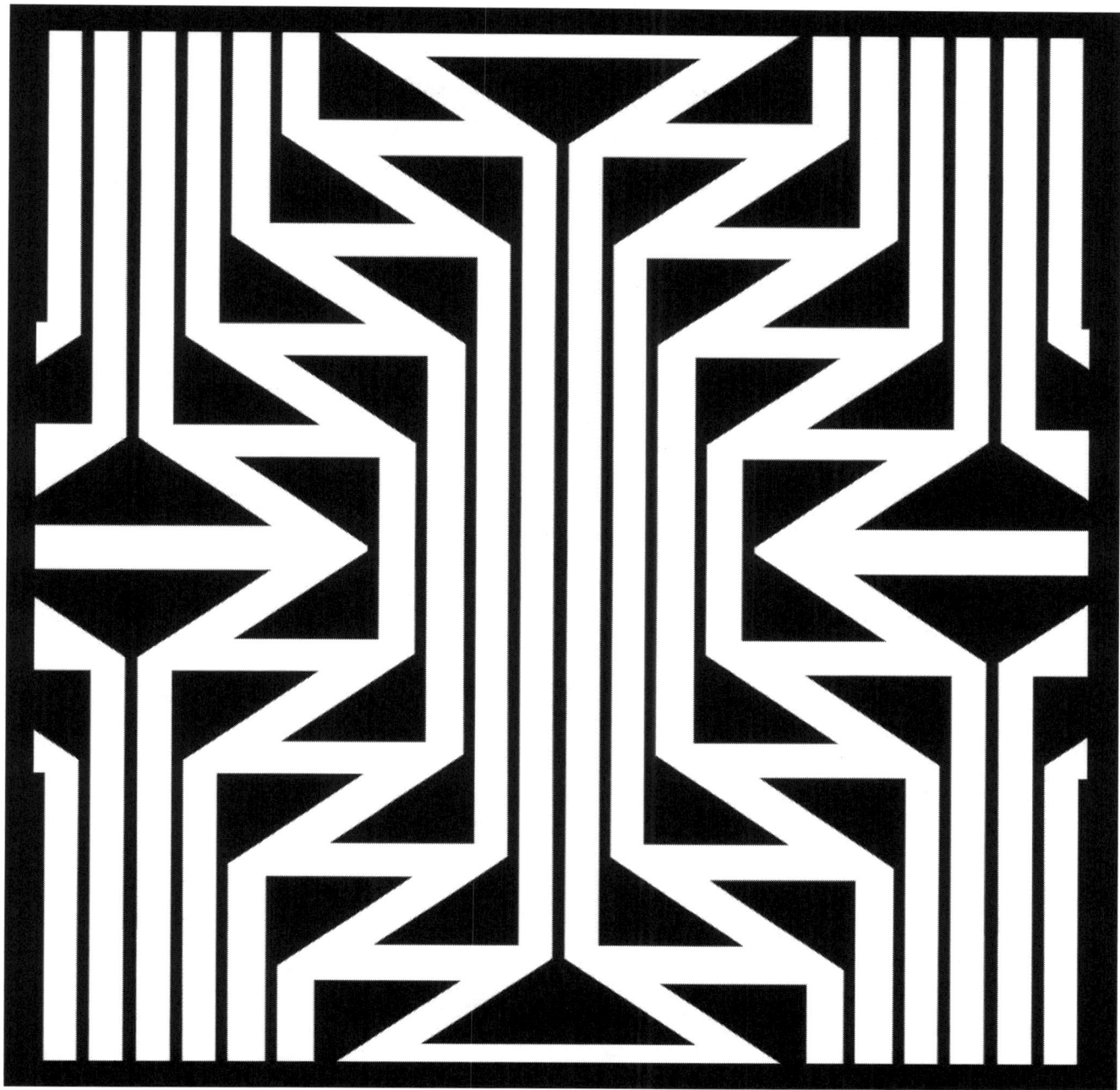

We Are The People – Naat A Maklaks

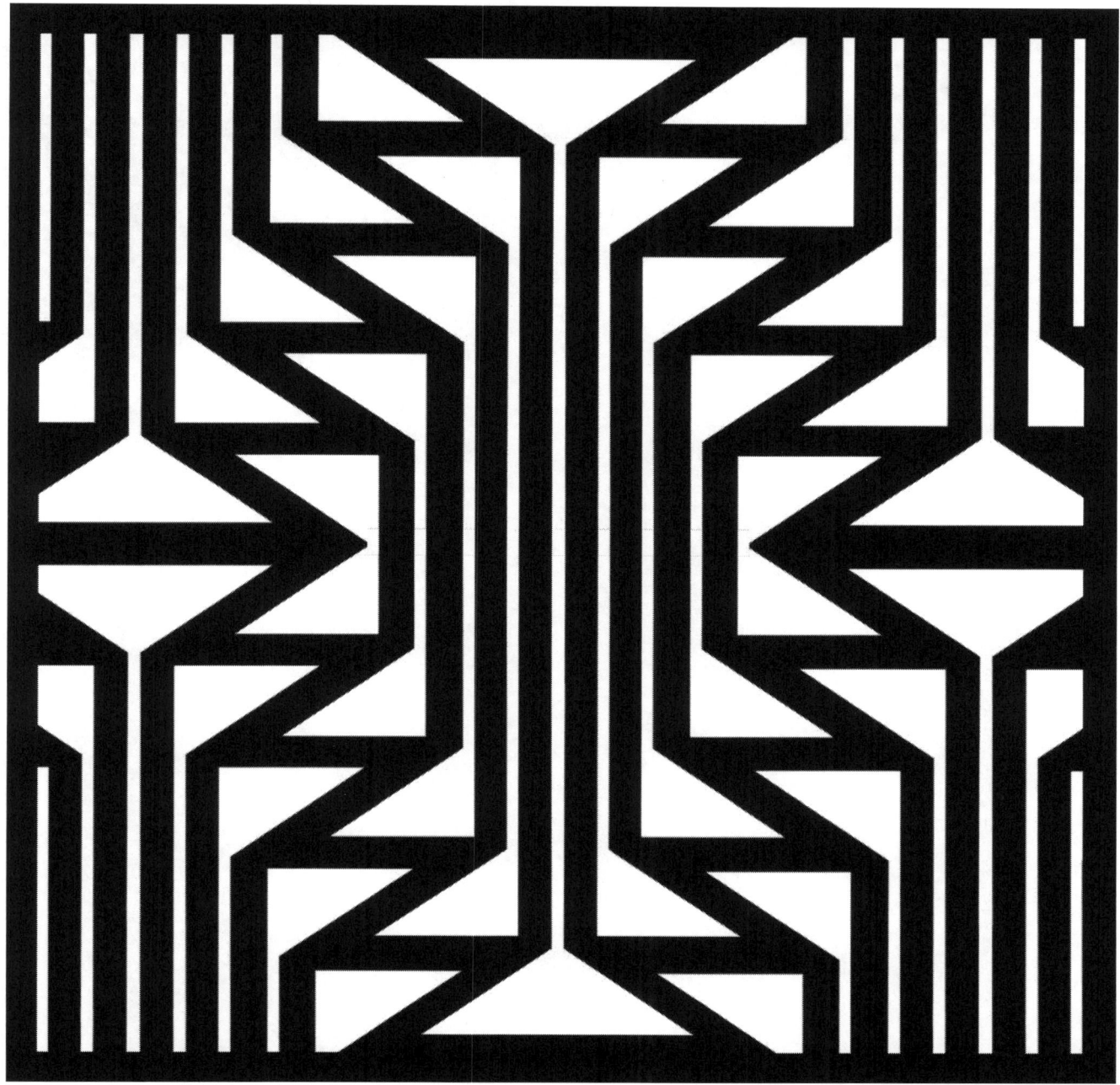

We Are The People – Naat A Maklaks

We Are The People – Naat A Maklaks

We Are The People – Naat A Maklaks

We Are The People – Naat A Maklaks

We Are The People – Naat A Maklaks

We Are The People – Naat A Maklaks

We Are The People – Naat A Maklaks

We Are The People – Naat A Maklaks

We Are The People – Naat A Maklaks

We Are The People – Naat A Maklaks

We Are The People – Naat A Maklaks

We Are The People – Naat A Maklaks

We Are The People – Naat A Maklaks

We Are The People – Naat A Maklaks

We Are The People – Naat A Maklaks

We Are The People – Naat A Maklaks

We Are The People – Naat A Maklaks

We Are The People – Naat A Maklaks

We Are The People – Naat A Maklaks

We Are The People – Naat A Maklaks

We Are The People – Naat A Maklaks

We Are The People – Naat A Maklaks

We Are The People – Naat A Maklaks

We Are The People – Naat A Maklaks

We Are The People – Naat A Maklaks

We Are The People – Naat A Maklaks

We Are The People – Naat A Maklaks

We Are The People – Naat A Maklaks

We Are The People – Naat A Maklaks

We Are The People – Naat A Maklaks

We Are The People – Naat A Maklaks

We Are The People – Naat A Maklaks

About The Author

Shuína Skó (pronounced "Shoo-in-uh Sk-oh") is a citizen of the Klamath Tribes located on the border of California and Oregon.

Their birth name is "Kayce Womack" and they go by their ewksiknii name "Shuína Skó," meaning "Singing Spring," to honor their culture and ancestors.

Shuína comes from the Marsh people, a group within the ewksiknii, led by their great-great-great-great-grandfather Chinchallo MukHas (Signer of the 1864 Klamath Treaty and healer).

Shuína is an internationally known self-published author, Two-Spirit spoken word poet, and Indigenous rights activist.

After completing a Bachelor of Science in Applied Psychology, Shuína went on to gain over 10 years of professional experience providing direct mental/behavioral health services to children and families within marginalized communities.

Shuína has performed spoken word poetry, facilitated workshops, and provided cultural consultation services throughout Turtle Island.

Books by Shuína Skó

Shuína's books elicit strong emotion and provoke thought. Their passion for sharing culture and uplifting vulnerable peoples is evident throughout these books. Shuína believes there is exponential power in storytelling and encourages each of us to share our story, too.

Indigenous Creations

This coloring book is a testament
of a vibrant, resilient, and innovative culture

The 75 coloring creations highlight traditional
basket designs along with several significant plants and animals
that are valuable relations of the ewksiknii

There are three distinct basket designs
repeated throughout, which include quail, mountain
or goose, and crow's knee

The plants and animals appearing in this book
are bear, buffalo, butterfly, deer, frog, hummingbird, coyote, quail,
eagle, cedar, sage, wocas (pond lily), and sugar pinecone

www.ShuinaSko.com

Made in United States
Troutdale, OR
03/17/2025

29825874R00102